I0821902

THE DUST BOWL

BY MARIE ROESSER

Gareth Stevens PUBLISHING

CRASHCOURSE

Please visit our website, www.garethstevens.com. For a free color catalog of all our high-quality books, call toll free 1-800-542-2595 or fax 1-877-542-2596.

Library of Congress Cataloging-in-Publication Data

Names: Roesser, Marie, author.
Title: The Dust Bowl / Marie Roesser.
Description: New York : Gareth Stevens Publishing, 2020. | Series: A look at US history | Includes index.
Identifiers: LCCN 2019010260| ISBN 9781538248713 (pbk.) | ISBN 9781538248737 (library bound) | ISBN 9781538248720 (6 pack)
Subjects: LCSH: Dust storms--Great Plains--History--20th century--Juvenile literature. | Great Plains--Social conditions--Juvenile literature. | Depressions--1929--Great Plains--Juvenile literature. | Agriculture--Great Plains--History--20th century--Juvenile literature. | Droughts--Great Plains--History--20th century--Juvenile literature. | Dust Bowl Era, 1931-1939--Juvenile literature.
Classification: LCC F595 .R695 2020 | DDC 978/.032--dc23
LC record available at https://lccn.loc.gov/2019010260

First Edition

Published in 2020 by
Gareth Stevens Publishing
111 East 14th Street, Suite 349
New York, NY 10003

Editor: Therese Shea

Photo credits: Series art Christophe BOISSON/Shutterstock.com; (feather quill) Galushko Sergey/Shutterstock.com; (parchment) mollicart-design/Shutterstock.com; cover, p. 1 NOAA George E. Marsh Album, theb1365, Historic C&GS Collection/Wikimedia; p. 5 Photoonlife/Shutterstock.com; p. 7 Bettmann/Getty Images; p. 9 U.S. National Archives and Records Administration/Wikimedia; p. 11 Everett Historical/Shutterstock.com; p. 13 PhotoQuest/Archive Photos /Getty Images; p. 15 Arthur Rothstein/Wikimedia; pp. 17, 21, 25 Universal History Archive/Universal Images Group/Getty Images; p. 19 Courtesy of the Library of Congress; p. 23 FPG/Hulton Archive/Getty Images; p. 27 Dorothea Lange/Hulton Archive/Getty Images; p. 29 iko/Shutterstock.com.

Printed in the United States of America

CPSIA compliance information: Batch #CW20GS: For further information contact Gareth Stevens, New York, New York at 1-800-542-2595.

CONTENTS

Words in the glossary appear in **bold** type the first time they are used in the text.

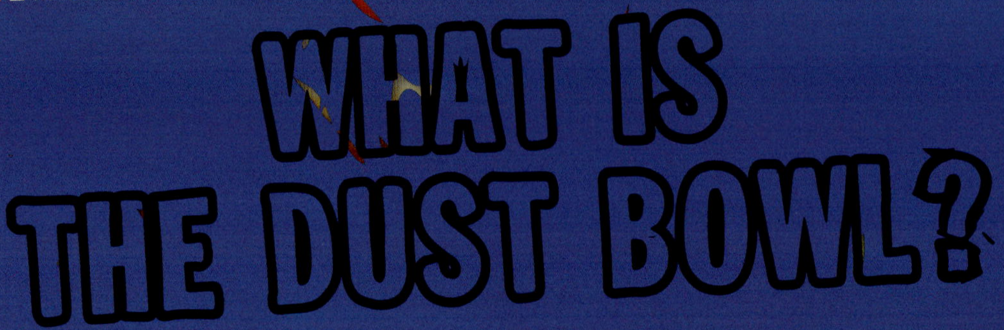

WHAT IS THE DUST BOWL?

The Dust Bowl was an area in the Great Plains of the United States in the 1930s. It had been grasslands, but became **barren**. Read on to find out how this happened and about the people who lived there through this hard time.

MAKE THE GRADE

The Dust Bowl hit parts of Colorado, Kansas, Texas, Oklahoma, and New Mexico hardest, but many more states were affected.

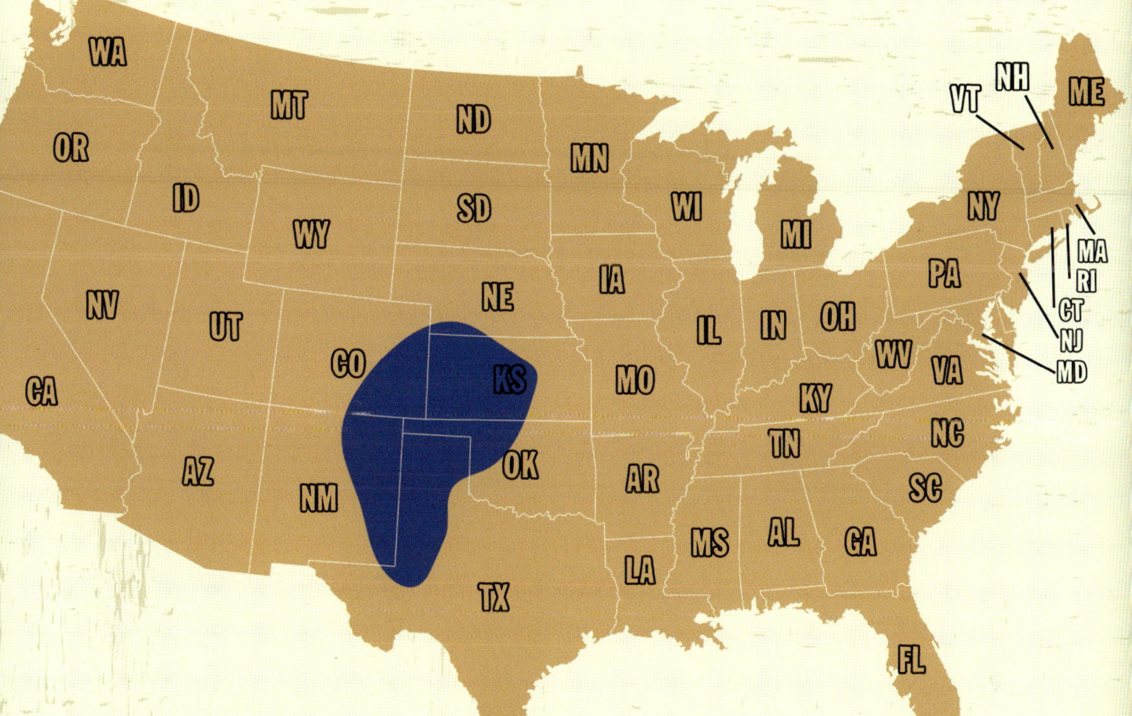

MOST AFFECTED BY DUST BOWL

CLEARING LAND

In the mid-1800s, the US government asked people to settle on the Great Plains. Some used the grasslands to raise livestock. Others cleared land to farm crops. In the early 1900s, wheat was in **demand**. More farmers began to clear land to grow wheat.

MAKE THE GRADE

World War I, fought from 1914 to 1918, was one reason for the wheat demand. Soldiers overseas needed bread to eat.

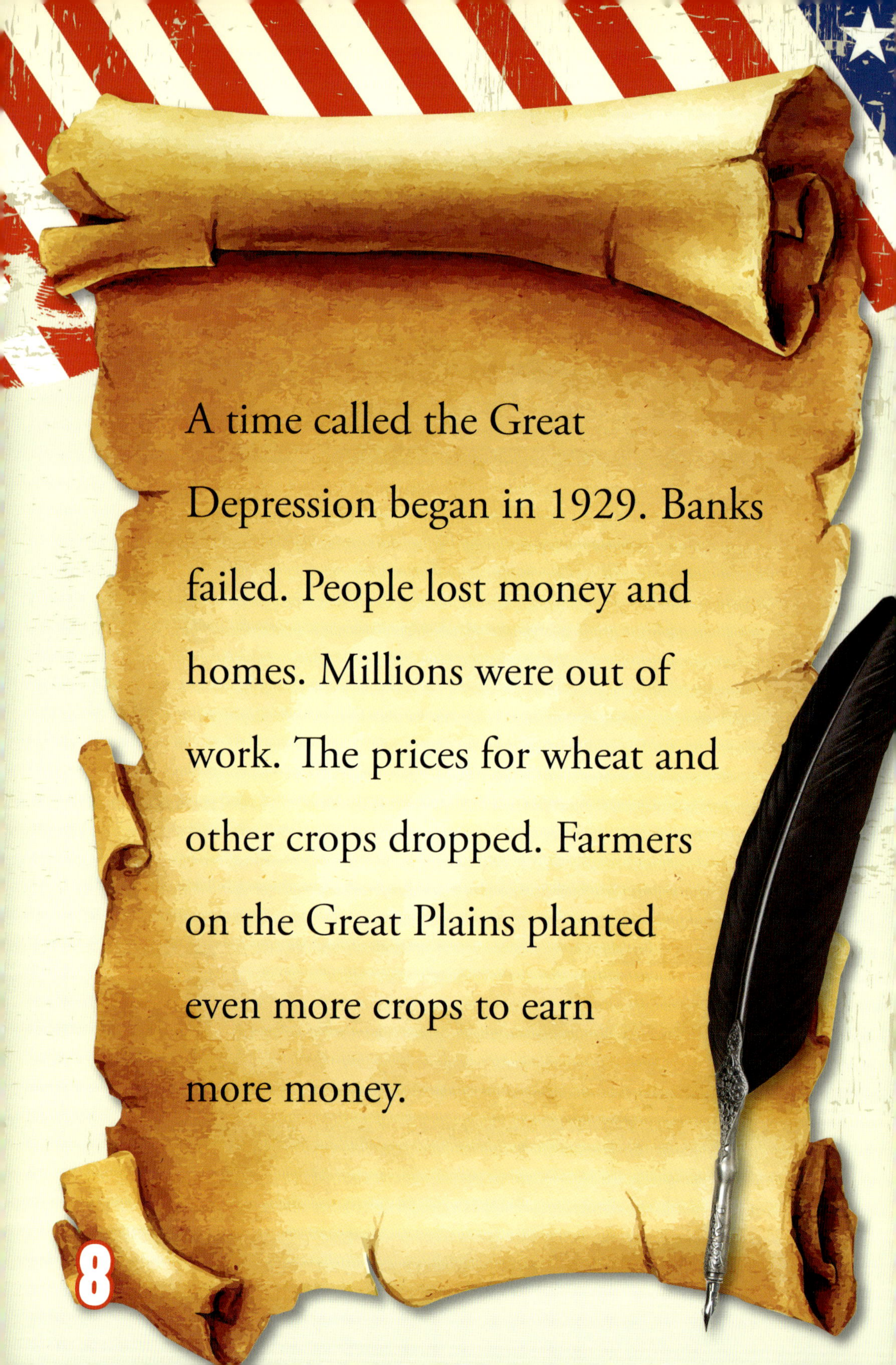

A time called the Great Depression began in 1929. Banks failed. People lost money and homes. Millions were out of work. The prices for wheat and other crops dropped. Farmers on the Great Plains planted even more crops to earn more money.

MAKE THE GRADE

The Great Depression continued until the United States entered World War II in 1941. The war created many new jobs.

DRYING UP

In the 1930s, the Great Plains had several **droughts**. The land dried up because of the lack of rain. Crops failed. So much grassland had been cleared that there weren't enough plants to hold the soil in place.

MAKE THE GRADE

Plant roots keep soil in place and also hold water.

BLACK BLIZZARDS

Winds blew through the Great Plains and picked up loose soil from dry farmland. Windstorms were called "black **blizzards**" because of the amount of dirt in the air. They blocked sunlight, sometimes for days, and carried dust to the East Coast.

MAKE THE GRADE

People became sick because of the dust in the air. They had chest pains and breathing problems. Hundreds—maybe thousands—died.

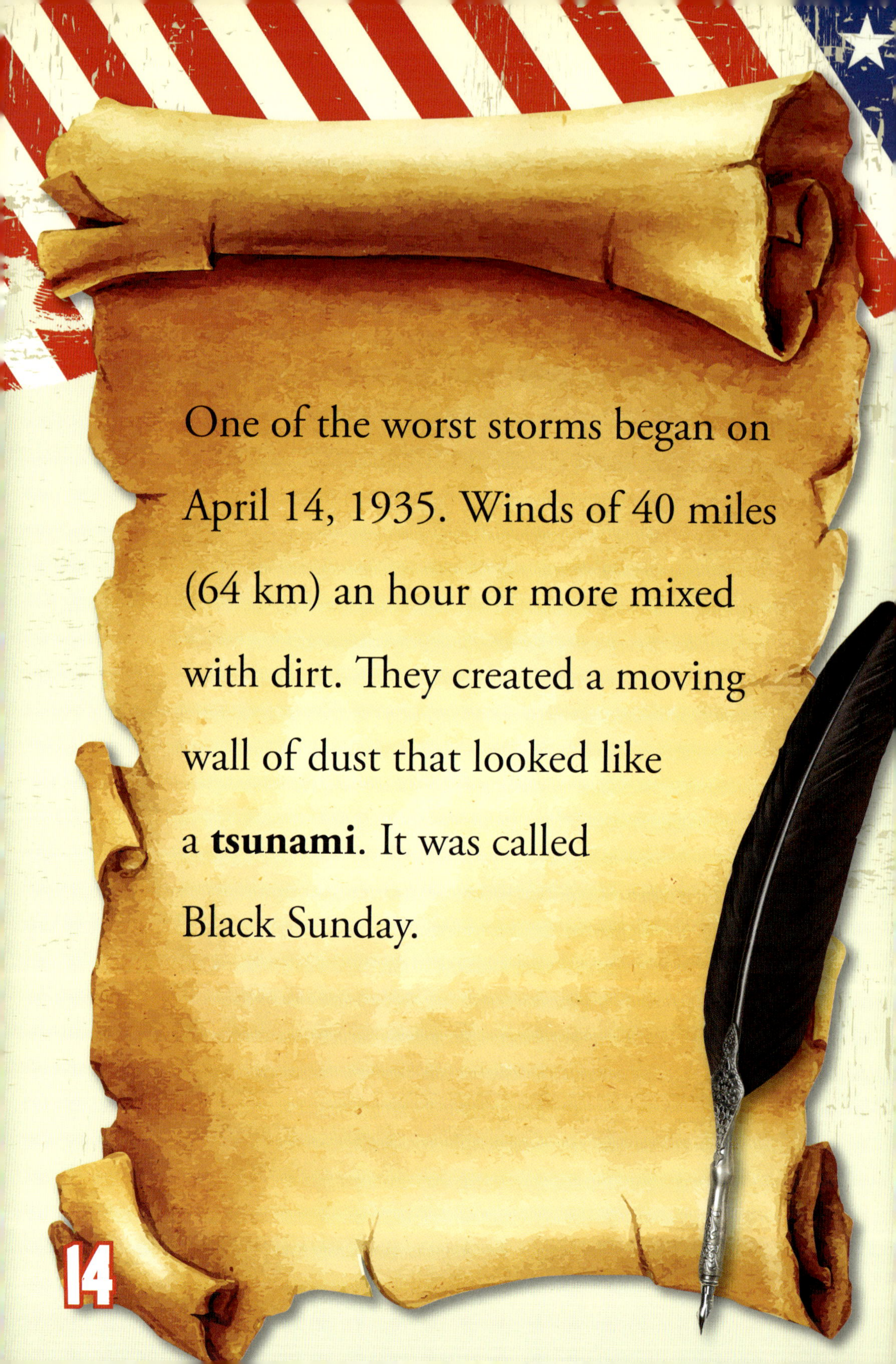

One of the worst storms began on April 14, 1935. Winds of 40 miles (64 km) an hour or more mixed with dirt. They created a moving wall of dust that looked like a **tsunami**. It was called Black Sunday.

MAKE THE GRADE

A news reporter writing about this terrible storm said it started in the "dust bowl." This was the first time these words were used to describe the area.

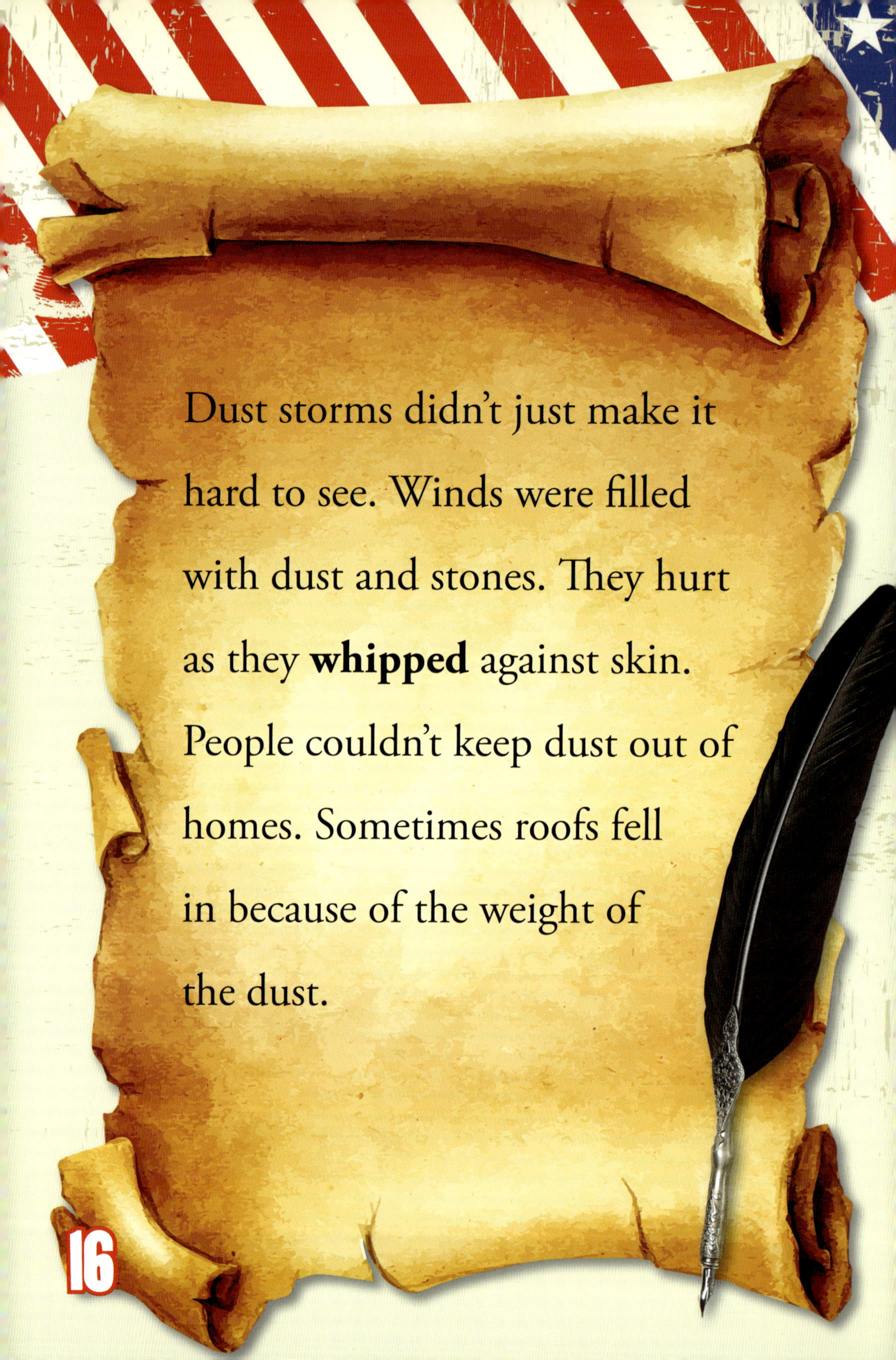

Dust storms didn't just make it hard to see. Winds were filled with dust and stones. They hurt as they **whipped** against skin. People couldn't keep dust out of homes. Sometimes roofs fell in because of the weight of the dust.

MAKE THE GRADE

Some people call the time of the Dust Bowl the "Dirty Thirties."

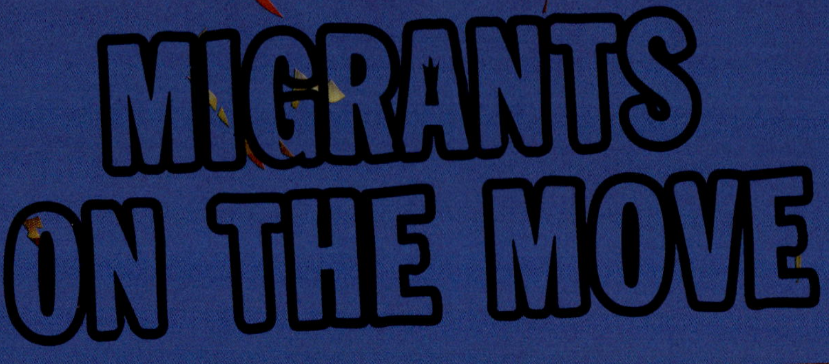

MIGRANTS ON THE MOVE

Finally, farmers and others in the Dust Bowl gave up. They needed food and money. By 1940, about 2.5 million had moved. Most went west to find work. However, with the Great Depression going on, there weren't many jobs.

MAKE THE GRADE

Photographer Dorothea Lange took many powerful pictures of people during the Dust Bowl and the Great Depression, like the famous one shown here.

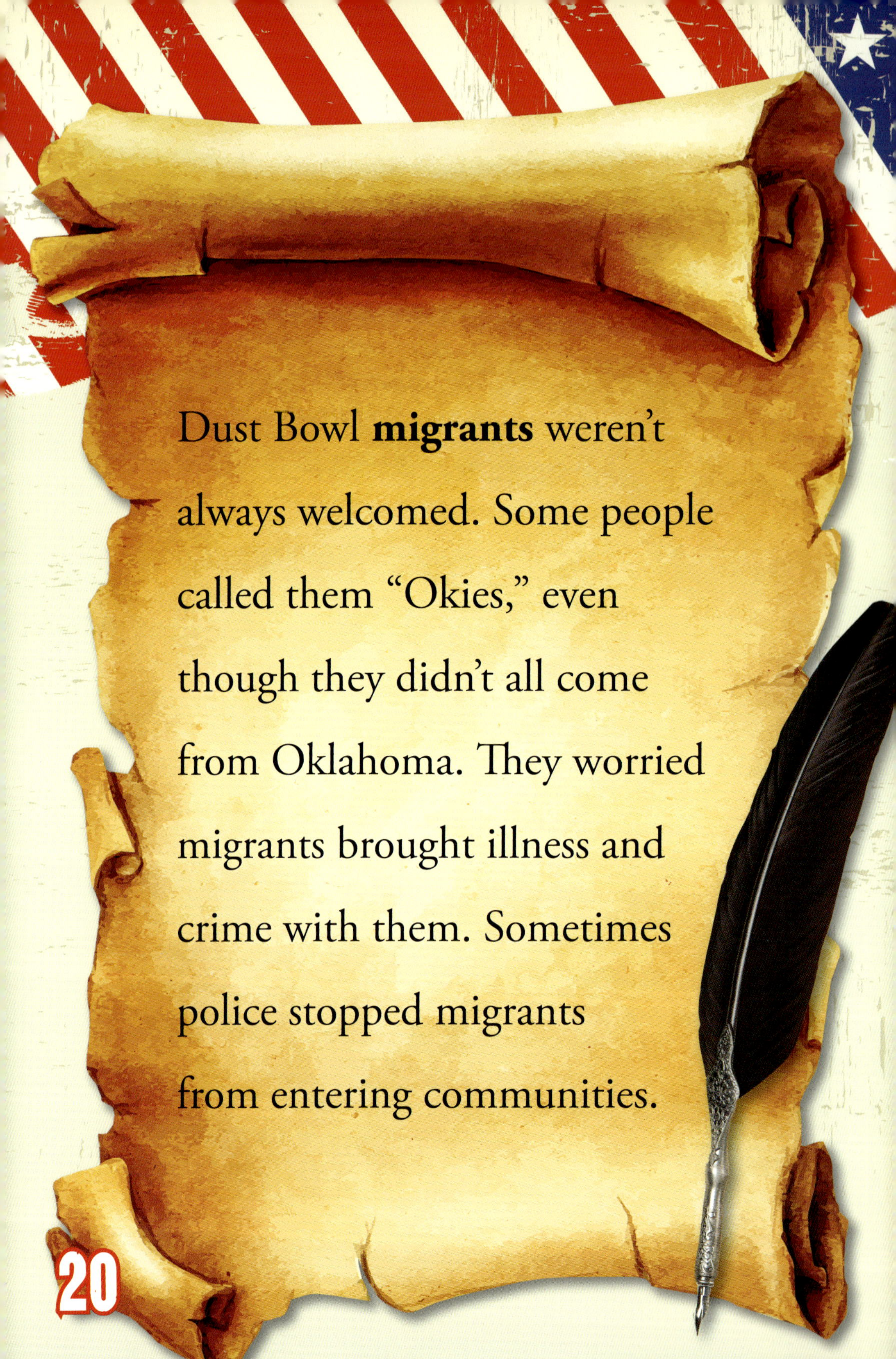

Dust Bowl **migrants** weren't always welcomed. Some people called them "Okies," even though they didn't all come from Oklahoma. They worried migrants brought illness and crime with them. Sometimes police stopped migrants from entering communities.

MAKE THE GRADE

Many migrants from the Dust Bowl had to live in tents or poorly built houses called shanties outside of farms and towns.

FIGHTING BACK

Franklin D. Roosevelt became US president in 1933. Beginning in 1935, millions of trees were planted to break the force of the winds across the Great Plains. The Soil **Conservation** Service taught new farming methods to fight the problem of soil **erosion**.

MAKE THE GRADE

The government gave farmers money to set aside land as grasslands and forests.

RECOVERY

When the United States entered World War II, many Dust Bowl migrants moved to cities. They took jobs making things that were needed in war, such as airplanes and ships. Rainfall returned to the Great Plains by the end of 1939. Farms **recovered**.

MAKE THE GRADE

It's believed around 400,000 people from the Dust Bowl went to California.

REMEMBERING THE DUST BOWL

The Dust Bowl is remembered through art. **Musicians**, such as Woody Guthrie, wrote songs about it. Writer John Steinbeck wrote about it in his book *The Grapes of Wrath*. The work of artists and photographers showed people's suffering from that time.

MAKE THE GRADE

Photographer Dorothea Lange lived with migrants from the Dust Bowl for a time.

LESSONS LEARNED

People have learned lessons about caring for the **environment** from the Dust Bowl. They learned about better farming practices and conservation. More droughts have struck the Great Plains since the 1930s. However, none have produced another Dust Bowl.

MAKE THE GRADE

Helping people during the Dust Bowl may have cost the government about $1 billion. That would be more than $18 billion today.

KEY DATES OF THE DUST BOWL

1929
The Great Depression begins.

1930
The first of many droughts of the Dust Bowl begins.

1931
The dust storms sometimes called black blizzards begin.

1933
Franklin D. Roosevelt becomes president.

1934
The Shelterbelt Project, later called the Prairie States Forestry Project, is founded to plant trees in the Great Plains.

1935
The Black Sunday dust storm occurs. The Soil Conservation Service teaches new farming methods.

1936
Dorothea Lange takes the photo *Migrant Mother, Nipomo, California*.

1939
John Steinbeck's book *The Grapes of Wrath* comes out. Drought ends in the Great Plains. Rainfall returns.

1940
About 2.5 million people had moved from the Great Plains by this year.

GLOSSARY

barren: having few plants

blizzard: a heavy snowstorm with strong winds

conservation: the care of the natural world

demand: a powerful need for something

drought: a long period of very dry weather

environment: the natural world in which a plant or animal lives

erosion: the act of wearing away by water, wind, or ice

migrant: a person who goes from one place to another often to find work

musician: one who plays, makes, or sings music

photographer: a person who takes pictures with a camera as a career

recover: to return to a normal state after a hard time

tsunami: a huge wave of water created by an underwater earthquake or volcano

whip: to move quickly or with force

FOR MORE INFORMATION

Books

Blake, Kevin. *Sick Soil: The Dust Bowl*. New York, NY: Bearport Publishing, 2018.

Loh-Hagan, Virginia. *Famine and Dust: Dust Bowl*. Ann Arbor, MI: 45th Parallel Press, 2019.

Websites

The Great Depression: Dust Bowl
ducksters.com/history/us_1900s/dust_bowl.php
Read more about this hard time in American history.

Timeline: The Dust Bowl
pbs.org/wgbh/americanexperience/features/dust-bowl-surviving-dust-bowl/
Read more about what happened each year of the Dust Bowl.

Publisher's note to educators and parents: Our editors have carefully reviewed these websites to ensure that they are suitable for students. Many websites change frequently, however, and we cannot guarantee that a site's future contents will continue to meet our high standards of quality and educational value. Be advised that students should be closely supervised whenever they access the internet.

INDEX